work, love, pray
study guide

4word®

4WORDWOMEN.ORG

To order additional copies of this resource:

Order online at 4wordwomen.org or email hello@4wordwomen.org

4word

To connect, lead and support professional Christian women to achieve their God-given potential.

In numbers far exceeding past generations, women today are earning advanced degrees and entering full-time careers while juggling relationships, families, church and community activities.

71% *of women with children under 18 are working outside the home.*

Professional women - single or married, parenting or not - must navigate a changed business culture that prizes intense career commitment over other priorities.

27% *of professional women are leaving church, feeling underutilized and isolated.*

With a scarcity of female mentors to model professional success balanced with integrated faith and healthy relationships, women are working in survival mode and dropping out of church in record numbers.

The only national organization serving professional Christian women, 4word is narrowing the gap in resources facing every woman serious about her career, relationships and faith.

connect busy working women face to face in local group gatherings, and in an active online community. 4word's Mentor Program connects women across the nation for mentoring with our proprietary curriculum.

lead today's professional women seeking balance while developing gifts with enormous potential to impact their families, companies, and church communities. The vision is cast in *Work, Love, Pray*, released in 2011 by business and mentoring thought leader Diane Paddison.

support with practical resources: outstanding digital content, inspiring interviews, and a curated resource directory at 4wordwomen.org. Partnerships with more than 200 like-minded organizations leverage our collective impact.

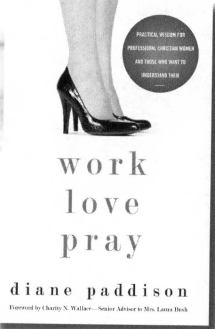

PRACTICAL WISDOM FOR PROFESSIONAL CHRISTIAN WOMEN AND THOSE WHO WANT TO UNDERSTAND THEM

work
love
pray

d i a n e   p a d d i s o n

Foreword by Charity N. Wallace—Senior Advisor to Mrs. Laura Bush

"I am confident you will find Work, Love, Pray inspiring and encouraging. When we stay close to God, we never know the exciting places he will take us. This book will prepare you to go."

Charity N. Wallace
Director, Women's Initiative, Bush Institute

The ratio of women in today's workforce is rising, and old best practices no longer apply. Women launching careers, those considering career transitions, and working mothers re-entering the marketplace will find wisdom for every life stage in Work, Love, Pray.

High-profile commercial real estate executive, corporate board director and mentoring expert Diane Paddison shares the ups and downs of her own corporate, personal, and spiritual life. 15 more leaders advise how to progress in your career without compromise. The foreword is authored by successful executive Charity Wallace, Senior Advisor to Mrs. Laura Bush and Director of the Bush Women's Initiative.

CONTENTS ::

A Word from the Author..7

A Word from the Editor..8

How to Use This Study Guide..9

Chapter 1: Dream Job...10

Chapter 2: Farm Girl..14

   :: Questions to Ask to Positively Impact and

   Empower Young Girls...18

Chapter 3: From Harrisburg..20

Chapter 4: Reality Sets In...24

Chapter 5: When Your World Collapses..................................30

Chapter 6: Single, Married... Whatever...................................36

   :: 5 Ways to Reach Out to and Embrace the

   Single Women in Your Life..40

Chapter 7: The Truth Will Open Some Doors... and Close Others............42

Chapter 8: Finding Compatible Work Environments.................48

Chapter 9: Trade on Your Strengths......................................52

Chapter 10: The Facts about Faith..58

Chapter 11: What about Church?.. 64

Chapter 12: Grow Your Faith Like You Grow Your Career.........68

   :: Spiritual Growth Self Test..70

   :: 6 Ways to Pray Throughout the Workday........................ 72

CONTENTS ::

Chapter 13: When You're Both Wearing the Pants.............................74

:: God's Minimum Standards of Finance...............................78

Chapter 14: A Little Help from Your Friends..............................80

:: 6 Ways to Embrace Your Femininity at Work...................83

Chapter 15: No One's Perfect...86

:: Are you a Perfectionist?...87

Chapter 16: Change with the Seasons.....................................92

Chapter 17: Set (and Observe) Your Boundaries.......................98

Chapter 18: Isn't This Fun?...102

Connect with 4word..106

Credits...107

To the woman that encourages and inspires me,

Welcome to the "Work, Love, Pray" Study Guide. My heart behind this study guide is for you to grow in community with other women. When I have gathered in community with women in my place of caring about God's use of me in relationship and at work, I have been able to support and encourage others as I have gone through this study and through life. I hope it does the same for you.

On page 3, we outline the mission and strategy of 4word: to connect, lead and support professional Christian women to achieve their God-given potential. You can join us online at 4wordwomen.org and through our Local Groups that meet in cities across the country. Women throughout the world have been touched as follows:

"Our group used the first chapter of [Work, Love, Pray] as the catalyst to discuss career decisions. It became a natural dialogue with women sharing different experiences and concerns. There is a strong desire for a supportive place for Christian working women and everyone wants the chance to meet often and become closer." – Keysha, San Francisco

"With 4word I experience lots of different kinds of community, but the most beneficial aspect for me has been finding a group of about 10 women who I have created really strong intentional bonds with. We meet twice a week together and have been able to really hear people's stories and their struggles. They understand where I'm at, including my struggles at work and my struggles in my relationships, and also my struggles with trying to grow in my faith. I don't have to hide any part of my life. I don't have to make anything smaller or minimize anything, I can just be me." – Maria, Portland

"What has probably been the most beneficial for me is that I recently found your 4word organization. I have thoroughly enjoyed the emails, blogs, article links, etc. They have been quite encouraging and are great reminders as to how Christ can and should infiltrate our lives in all aspects – whether at home or at work." – Lisa, Dallas

Again, I hope you find a wonderful group of women who you can trust and build authentic relationships with as you go through my book "Work, Love, Pray" and this study guide.

May you be blessed,

Diane Paddison

Founder, 4wordwomen.org

Author, "Work, Love, Pray

We're so thrilled you've picked up this study guide as a companion to Diane's amazing book, Work, Love, Pray. Since it was published, we have had the amazing opportunity to participate in book studies and discussions around the country on what it means to be a woman that strives to work and love and pray.....every day.....even when we feel alone and overwhelmed. We developed this guide to support communities of like-minded women who are balancing the three-legged stool of career, relationships, and faith.

I was raised by hard-working parents in South Louisiana. When I landed my dream job out of college, I tried to work harder than everyone else, had no hobbies, and tirelessly strived for achievement at all costs. After a steep climb up the corporate ladder with the "no pets, no plants" rule, I had everything I thought I had ever wanted. I now realize that I spent years putting on masks, labels, and layers to cover up who I really was.....a small town girl raised with chickens, tractors, hand-me-down clothes, and the insecurity that I was never good enough. I had layered on degrees, job titles, stuff, awards, and more stuff to portray an image that I thought the world wanted to see.

While I stood on a Manhattan street on 9/11, I realized the title on my business card and the number of digits on my paycheck did not matter at all. After that day, those layers began to fall off. Some quickly but some slow and painfully. What emerged was a young peacock who was proud of who she was and her differences. She wasn't a penguin who worked hard to dress, talk, walk, and dream like others just to fit into their club. Vulnerability was no longer a bad thing. I let others in, and I liked it.

Since then, I have gotten married, survived cancer, and faced the challenges of infertility and the subsequent losses that followed. Jeff and I have now been married 10 years and have three amazing children that are the light of my life. Before I read the book, I felt very alone in my career pursuits and attempts to juggle being a mother, wife, daughter, sister, and friend. When we are in the thick of the fray, we often feel we are isolated. Once I read the book, I realized there are a lot of us out there whose calling is to work OUTSIDE of the home while still RUNNING the home.

I have learned that you don't have to go through all the yucky things in search of what the world calls success. The world's definition of success will not satisfy. Authenticity and transparency, with yourself and others, are the two of the most important things in life. Being genuine and vulnerable will open the door to meaningful relationships and a meaningful life...and YOUR definition of success will become apparent.

I sincerely hope, in any small way, that this study guide helps you shed your layers of labels and be the amazing you that the Lord created you to be.

With love and support,

Sandra Crawford Williamson, 4word COO

 4word

How to Use This Study Guide

:: Individual Study

Read each chapter of Work, Love, Pray and then answer the questions in this study guide. Dig deeper with the Scriptures and prayer prompts that accompany each chapter.

:: Small Groups

Before each meeting, read the chapter of Work, Love, Pray. Go through the questions in the guide and be prepared to discuss and answer the questions with your group. When you meet together, read the Scriptures for the chapter, discuss and answer the questions, and pray through the prayer prompts at the end of the chapter.

:: Large Groups

Before each meeting, read the chapter of Work, Love, Pray and answer the questions for the chapter. When you meet together, read the Scriptures for the chapter, discuss the chapter and your answers to the questions, and pray through the prayer prompts with each other.

While this study guide can be used on your own, we suggest using it in a group setting. It is important to have community with other women where you can support and encourage one another.

When using this study guide in a group setting, remember to practice confidentiality, be authentic, show grace and forgiveness to one another, and respect each other's opinions. Don't try to give advice unless someone asks for it, but always ask good questions!

If you are using this guide with a small group, let us know at hello@4wordwomen.org! You can get ongoing content suggestions, and we can add you to our email list for blogs and other materials.

REFLECTION

Describe your dream job and ideal balance of career, faith, and personal or family lifestyle (whether single, dating, married, divorced; with children or without)?

READ

:: Colossians 3:1-2

:: Proverbs 3:5-6

:: 2 Chronicles 15:7

Are you happy with the balance in your work, personal life, and faith right now? What would you like to change?

What are your guidelines/goals for balancing work, family and faith?

 4word

What are your career deal breakers- those things that would keep you from taking a job or that would cause you to quit a job?

What would you be willing to give up in order to have your dream job? Would you be willing to relocate, take a cut in pay, seek additional training?

When you have a major decision to make, how do you go about making it? What are some influences that impact your decision-making? What role does your faith play in the process?

Diane describes her conversation with John where she speaks up about her commitments to her family, marriage, and faith. How would you bring up your concerns about family and faith in a similar situation?

 4word

ACTION

What are your priorities and values?

 NOTES

Diane writes that, "It's one thing to say that your family and your faith are more important to you than your career. Values are easy to hold when they're never challenged. But when push comes to shove, you learn whether they really are the guiding priorities of your life." Are your priorities and values reflected in your actions each day? If not, how can you change that?

PRAY

:: Ask for God's strength and discernment in how you spend your time.

:: Ask God if your values and priorities are in line with His plan for your life.

:: Ask God for wisdom and direction in your decisions, whether these are daily decisions at work or major life decisions.

:: Talk to God about the difficulties you have in practically living out your priorities.

NOTES

 4word

REFLECTION

What events or experiences in your childhood and youth do you feel had a positive influence on you? Explain.

READ

:: Psalm 119:1-3

:: Proverbs 13:20

:: Mark 7:20-23

:: Romans 5:3-5

:: 1 Timothy 4:12

What are you doing to build on those positive experiences? How have they helped you in your career?

Proverbs 17:17 says, "As iron sharpens iron, so one man sharpens another" (NIV). Are you teachable? Who in your life has influenced and sharpened you?

Describe a specific situation in your personal life, career, or faith journey that produced valuable skills you now use, or qualities you have developed?

NOTES

What have you learned from your work experiences?

Not all experiences are positive. How can you find and apply lessons from negative experiences in life? How does your faith help in this process?

Diane says that her parents and farm life instilled self-discipline in her at a very early age. This is a characteristic that has made her very successful. Are there younger people in your life who may be watching and learning from you? if so, what are they learning?

 4word®

Romans 8:28 says, "And we know that in all things God works for the good of those who love him, who have been called according to his purpose" (NIV). Surveying your own life, how do you see evidence of this?

NOTES

ACTION

What gets you excited? Does your work take advantage of the things you naturally loved to do as you grew up? If not, what can you do to change that?

What are you doing to overcome the negative influences from your past?

What can you do to be a better example to those around you?

PRAY

:: Thank God for the godly influences in your life.

:: Ask God to help you delight in Him no matter what the circumstances.

:: Ask God for wisdom to be a positive influence and example to others.

:: Talk to God about how to overcome past and present negative influences in your life.

NOTES

 4word

Questions to Ask to Positively Impact and Empower Young Girls

Young girls look up to you and watch how you live your life. It is important to be aware of how you can positively impact these girls through your words. You can empower them through the questions you ask and the conversations you have with them. Here are some examples of meaningful questions you can ask:

What are you learning in school?

What is your favorite school subject?

Are you on any teams?

What book are you reading? What is your favorite book?

What is your favorite animal? Why?

If you could travel anywhere in the world, where would you like to go?

NOTES

4word

REFLECTION

What was your most difficult challenge in college? How did it affect your experience there?

READ

:: 2 Timothy 1:7

:: Titus 2:7-8

:: Philippians 4:13

:: Proverbs 17:17

:: Proverbs 22:1

What role did faith or spirituality play in your life prior to college? Did it change during your college years? Explain.

Identify at least two things you learned about yourself during your college experience.

Were friendships a major part of your college experience?
How did your friendships impact your life?

NOTES

How do you network with people you would like to keep
in contact with?

What are some lessons or skills that you learned through
extracurricular activities?

What professional skills or lessons did you learn from
experiences in college?

 4word

What advice would you give to young women in college today?

NOTES

ACTION

Who are the people in your life that share your focus on faith, family, and profession and know you very well?

If the list is nonexistent or very short, what can you do to change that?

REFLECTION

:: Thank God for providing good godly friends and/or family. If you don't have this, ask God to provide a good godly friend.

:: Ask God how you can serve and be a good influence to others in your life.

:: Pray for your friends specifically.

:: Talk to God about the struggles you are facing in your current friendships or family.

NOTES

4word

REFLECTION

If you are single, are you feeling pressured to find a husband?

How do you deal with that expectation?

Do you feel pressure from others to focus on your career first?

Do you feel you need to gain the approval of others? If so, why? How can your natural desire to be liked or to meet expectations be positive? When does it become unhealthy?

READ

:: 2 Corinthians 6:14

:: Psalm 112

:: Philippians 4:6-12

:: Hebrews 13:5

:: Proverbs 16:9

NOTES

Diane says, "If you have convictions that cut against the grain of your work world, be prepared to have them challenged. But I've also learned that if you consistently hold on to those convictions and take the time to explain the reasons behind them, you will gain the respect of your colleagues, even if they never fully agree with you." When you are faced with a challenge from a colleague about your convictions, can you clearly explain the reasons behind them?

Do you feel you have a life-giving circle of friends and mentors? Do you find meaning and purpose in your work and relationships? If not, why not?

Diane writes that "God speaks to us in many ways, and often he uses other people to assist him." How has God placed and used people in your life to speak to you and guide your steps?

Proverbs 3:5-6 tells us, "Trust in the Lord with all your heart and lean not on your own understanding; in all your ways acknowledge him, and he will make your paths straight." What are some situations where you trusted God and did not depend on your own understanding? How did God work through those situations?

How have you seen God's timing at work in your life?

ACTION

If you are married, are you and your husband discussing how to meet both of your goals for faith, family, and career?

Is your career and place of work nurturing your life goals? If not, what are you doing to address that situation? Have you included prayer in your daily decisions?

NOTES

Are you currently facing a situation where you need to depend fully on God and trust Him? How can you stop leaning on your own understanding and lean on His understanding?

PRAY

:: Thank God for His acceptance and love for you.

:: Ask for God's peace and contentment in this current life stage.

:: If you are single, ask for God's discernment in romantic relationships. Are the men you date as serious about their faith as you are about yours?

:: Talk to God about any attitudes that you sense are unhealthy, like an excessive desire for approval or security that weakens your judgment or boundaries. Ask Him to equip you to make difficult decisions.

NOTES

NOTES

4word

REFLECTION

What comes to mind when you hear the word "divorce"?

Being open about divorce and other life events that may be seen as "failures" is not easy. Are there parts of your story that are difficult to talk about? Can you relate to the author's struggle to tell her story?

The author advises those who have experienced divorce to focus on the good. Do you think it is possible to find something good in every bad situation in life? Reflect on some bad situations from your own life and the good things that have come from them.

READ

:: Proverbs 3:5

:: Matthew 11:28-30

:: 1 Peter 5:6-7

:: Philippians 4:19

:: 2 Corinthians 1:3-7

 4word

When you are experiencing difficult times of stress or sadness, what is the value of supportive friendships?

NOTES

During hard times, do you believe God is punishing you, or do you sense His presence with you?

Despite her divorce, the author still believes in marriage. Do you? What are your honest thoughts about marriage? Do the statistics about divorce frighten or discourage you?

How has your faith or family tradition influenced your thoughts about marriage and divorce?

Do you think it is possible to place too much emphasis on marriage? Why or why not?

Diane lists some guiding principles when it comes to dating:

- Don't be in a hurry.

- Beware long-distance romance.

- Pay attention.

- Do your due diligence.

- Go with your gut.

- Be honest with yourself.

If you are currently dating or considering dating, which of these principles stands out to you? Which might you need to pay attention to? If you are married, which principles would you most suggest to the single women in your life? Can you think of any other dating principles that you would recommend to single women?

 4word

If you are engaged or are about to become engaged, consider the three "why" questions that Diane asks. Why am I getting married? Why am I marrying this man? Why am I marrying this man now?

NOTES

ACTION

Who would you go to for support if you experienced a serious emotional trauma such as divorce, the loss of a loved one, or the unexpected loss of a job? Why? Does that person have a foundation of faith as they deal with life issues in addition to their own resources?

If the list is nonexistent or very short, what can you do to change that?

 4word

PRAY

:: Thank God for allowing difficult challenges in your life to shape you.

:: Ask God to help you see things from His perspective.

:: Ask God to show you the value and blessing of marriage.

:: Talk to God about the struggles you are currently facing.

NOTES

In what ways do you think contemporary culture has shaped your view of singleness and marriage? Are those views different from the views of your parents? Explain.

:: Romans 12:1-5, 9-19

:: Philippians 4:11-13

:: Ephesians 5

:: 2 Corinthians 6:14

:: 1 Corinthians 6

How do you think God views marriage?

Single men in their thirties are often said to have a fear of commitment. Is this a distinctly male issue or do you think women in the same age range have a similar fear? Why?

What are some of the qualities you most admire in a husband? Why?

Among the married people you know, who do you most admire for the way they live out their marriage? How would you describe their marriages?

After looking at the scripture passages, what is the culture's view of sex vs. God's view of sex? Why do you think He established those standards? Are there some standards that God calls us to that seem unreasonable or too hard to comply with in today's society?

If single, do you tend to date people with a similar interest in spiritual things? Do you look for a comparable maturity or sense they feel accountable to God for their own personal and spiritual growth?

 4word

ACTION

NOTES

According to 2010 U.S. Demographics data on America's Families and Living Arrangements, 43.6 percent of the U.S. popoulation are unmarried adults, and 44.9 percent of those adults are women (Source: http://www.christianpost.com/news/pew-for-one-how-is-the-church-responding-to-growing-number-of-singles-70586/). What could you do to help the church do a better job serving single women?

Why do both Christians and non-Christians have difficulty staying married? What can you do to improve your odds of divorce?

Scripture speaks of wisdom in counsel. Who do you know that would offer candid, wise advice on relationship difficulties or questions? Are you respectful of your partner's reputation by choosing trustworthy confidants, or do you find yourself complaining inappropriately about relationship issues to those who may not be discreet?

What things would you be willing to try to tune up your relationship with your boyfriend or husband?

NOTES

PRAY

:: Thank God for the strong Christian marriages you know.

:: Ask God how you can help your church reach out to single women in your area.

:: Ask God how you can better serve your boyfriend, husband, or those around you.

:: Talk to God about your fears, challenges, hopes, and struggles in singleness, marriage, or dating.

5 Ways to Reach Out to and Embrace the Single Women in Your Life

NOTES

Ask her about her life and work. Listen to her and follow up on the things going on in her life.

Celebrate the things and events that are important to her. If she gets a promotion, receives an award, or graduates, throw her a party! Don't hesitate to celebrate with her.

Invite her into your home and spend time with her away from your spouse and children. Make her feel welcome!

Share with her how God is working in your life, and not just in your shared life with your husband. Be open and honest about your own personal struggles and spiritual growth.

Be aware of the insecurities that single women face. Don't try to "fix" her singleness. Instead, speak identity into her. Share with her the God-given strengths and gifts that you see in her. She is a daughter of the King. Don't let her lose sight of her worth in Him.

4word

To what extent do you think a company should support or accomodate its employees' personal values?

:: Matthew 6:33

:: Colossians 1:16-17

:: Luke 1:37

:: Proverbs 22:4

Assuming that you desire to have a career that does not sacrifice your family, what are some specific expectations you would have of your employer?

:: Luke 12:22-31

:: 1 Timothy 6:6-10

In your own job experience, have you felt the pressure of conflicting high demands from both your family and job?

Have you ever brought up your convictions about family during an interview? Have you ever hidden those convictions out of fear?

 4word

NOTES

Diane says, "I've always felt that if I'm going to establish boundaries between my work and my faith and my family, I need to make sure that when I am at work, I give 110 percent." Can you relate to her statement? Do you feel that you are fully present and committed while at work?

When faced with a decision between sticking to your priorities and getting a job that is absolutely necessary for your family, how would you weigh the options? What would you tell your family in those circumstances?

Your daughter is singing a solo in her high school choir concert which falls on the same night that your boss wants you to join him and a key potential customer for dinner. What are your options, and how would you present them to your boss? To your family?

 4word

If you were the CEO of a company, what kind of policy would you put into place for employees who wanted to leave work early to watch their kids' sports activities?

 NOTES

In most two-income families, the woman - by an overwhelming majority - assumes primary responsibility for nurturing children and doing household chores such as cooking and laundry. Why do you think this is true? Is it biblical, cultural, or gender-driven?

ACTION

If you have children, how much time each day do you sit and talk with them, giving them your undivided attention? How would it affect your daily schedule if you made that a high priority?

 4word

What are your boundaries? How much are you willing to travel? Work late in the evening? What can you do to negotiate some boundaries, even in the face of long-established expectations of others with similar responsibilities?

NOTES

What do you think God wants from you regarding work and family?

ACTION

:: Thank God for your family and friends.

:: Pray for the Lord's guidance in helping you identify some options that would enable you to spend more time with your family.

:: Pray for your family members by name and about their specific needs.

:: Talk to God about balancing priorities.

:: Ask God how you can better serve your family.

NOTES

NOTES

<u>study guide</u> chapter **8**

 4word

REFLECTION

Given your current status (single, married, small children, etc.), describe your ideal work environment. Looking ahead to the next five or ten years, how might that ideal change?

READ

:: 1 Timothy 6:6-11

:: Proverbs 31

:: Proverbs 2

:: Colossians 3:22-23

:: Proverbs 11:16

Diane writes that "a company may have all the right policies for you as a working mom and still be unsupportive because of its personality." What is your current company's "personality"? What is the attitude towards soon-to-be new mothers, women with young children, etc?

What specific family-friendly policies are available to you at your current place of employment?

The author believes that family-friendly policies are privileges to earn rather than rights the company owes to its employees. Do you agree or disagree? Explain.

Would you feel comfortable talking with your employer about issues of family stress? Why or why not?

Finish this sentence: "My supervisor would not want to lose me because..." (If you have trouble completing the sentence, assess what steps you might take to become a more valuable employee.)

ACTION

Are you currently in a work environment that does not align with your values? If so, what steps can you take towards finding a more compatible workplace?

If you do not have children but hope to eventually, what privileges do you need to earn [at work] in order to maintain a good work/life balance while working and raising children?

PRAY

:: Thank God for the job you have and for providing for you.

:: If your workplace supports your values, thank God for helping you to be in a place that will allow you to maintain a healthy work/life balance.

:: If your workplace does not support your values, ask for God's discernment in finding a compatible workplace environment that supports your values.

:: Ask for wisdom in living out your values at work and for guidance in setting your priorities.

NOTES

 4word

Reflect back on your most recent performance review. How much time was spent reviewing your strengths? How much on your weaknesses? In what ways could a performance review be an opportunity for you to trade more on your strengths at your company?

READ

:: Psalm 139:1-16, 23-24

:: Ephesians 2:10

:: Genesis 1:27

:: Philippians 4:13

:: 2 Corinthians 12

:: Exodus 4:10-11

Have you ever taken any online assessments or professionally administered assessments? What did you learn about yourself? Have you found ways to apply your greatest strengths at work?

In addition to your classwork and major field of study in college, what other activities did you pursue because you had a strong interest in them? What was it about those activities that appealed to you? How could those interests translate into the type of work for which you would be best suited?

NOTES

In order for you to advance in your company, will you be moving more in the direction of your strengths or more in the direction of your weaknesses?

If a promotion meant that you would be doing things in which you had little interest or that did not maximize your strengths, what would you do? In conjunction with evaluating your strengths in a new role, have you considered your priorities in life and how the new opportunity fits with what you value most in your life?

ACTION

Make a list of ten skills or things that you do well. (Not just right now, but think back to when you were in junior high, high school, and college.) Now, go back and circle two or three that you do extremely well. How do you use those two or three things in your current job?

NOTES

What specific things will you do over the next six months to gain a clearer understanding of your strengths?

Consider finding a mentor through a program like the 4word Mentor Program (http://www.4wordwomen. org/sites/mentormatch/). Consider taking an online assessment or professionally administered assessment to uncover your strengths and weaknesses.

PRAY

NOTES

:: Thank God for His unwavering love and acceptance for you (no matter what your strengths and weaknesses are.)

:: Thank God for making you in His image and giving you the skills you need to do your job.

:: Ask God to give you confidence and also keep you humble.

:: Talk to God about any insecurities you have.

:: Ask God to give you the courage to seek out opportunities at work to build on your strengths.

4word

NOTES

NOTES

4word

Who were the people in your life that seemed to draw you to a belief in God?

:: Luke 3:12-13

:: Ephesians 5:8

:: Matthew 5:16

:: 1 Peter 2:12

:: Romans 12:2

What was it about them and their faith that made them appealing to you?

:: Romans 13:13

:: Colossians 4:6

What are some of the negative attitudes towards Christianity that you have observed from your friends and colleagues?

Why do you think people have these attitudes?

NOTES

2 Corinthians 5:17 says, "Therefore, if anyone is in Christ, he is a new creation; the old has gone, the new has come!" Becoming a Christian involves surrendering every part of ourselves to God. Have you surrendered the work aspects of your life to Him? If not, what can you do to surrender that part of your life?

Colossians 3:23 says, "Whatever you do, work at it with all your heart, as working for the Lord, not for men." At work, you serve God through serving your employer. Have you been working well with the mindset of serving the Lord through your job? If not, how will a change in your mindset affect how you work and your relationship with God?

Consider your colleagues from work. Do you take an interest in their wellbeing- personally, professionally, and spiritually? Are you aware of their religious beliefs? Have your actions in the workplace demonstrated your faith while respecting others' religious beliefs?

 4word

"Even if a colleague asks you one of those "wide open door" questions that invites you to talk about faith, think before you speak." Have you ever been in one of these situations? What did you say? What would you say in the future?

ACTION

What can you do to become more approachable at work so others will feel open to conversations about faith?

In what ways are you "living the example?" How would your colleagues know about your faith? Are there areas of integrity you need to address –gossip, expense tracking, attitudes about coworkers, etc. – to better represent what you believe?

PRAY

NOTES

:: Pray for God to use you in your workplace for Him.

:: If your workplace is hostile to Christianity, ask God for guidance and wisdom in your particular situation.

:: Ask God to give you opportunities and wisdom around sharing faith stories with your coworkers.

:: Thank God for the people in your life that drew you to belief in God.

NOTES

NOTES

4word

What do you like about your church? What's missing that would make it a better fit?

READ

:: Hebrews 13:7

:: Hebrews 10:25

:: Ephesians 4:1-3

:: Colossians 3:12-15

If there was a time you attended church as a young single adult, what was that experience like? What was your church's singles ministry like? How did married women relate to you? Is there anything you wish the church had done differently in the singles ministry?

Have you ever stopped attending church? What was it that led you to quit?

 4word

As a professional Christian woman, what spiritual needs do you have that you think might be unique to you?

What issues do you face that a stay-at-home mom wouldn't relate to?

ACTION

Do you know other working women like you at church? What do you wish your church would do for you as a professional woman? Why is this important to you?

If you have not already expressed this need, ask for a meeting with your pastor or a church leader to discuss this. You could be a critical voice for the working women in their community whose distinct interests and needs are not on the church leaders' radar.

What could you do to help address the needs of the other professional women in your church? How can you build community with them?

 NOTES

PRAY

:: Ask God what you could do to address the needs of professional women in your church.

:: Pray that God would enable you to meet other professional women in your church that you do not yet know.

:: Thank God for your church and pray for your church leaders and pastors.

:: If you do not go to church, ask God to help you find a church and community where you can grow and learn God's Word.

:: Ask God how you can encourage and reach the women in your church.

REFLECTION

What are your biggest challenges to maintaining a strong, dynamic faith?

READ

:: James 1:2-3

:: Romans 5:3-5

:: John 16:33

:: Proverbs 21:5

:: Proverbs 13:4

:: Psalm 145

Do you agree that when it comes to faith, family, and career, faith is usually the easiest to ignore? Why do you think this is?

Have you experiences any "storms" in your life so far? If so, what kinds of things helped you weather those storms?

 4word

What types of activities do you try to engage in as a way of growing your faith?

What do you think of when you hear the word "discipline"? Do you consider yourself to be a person who enjoys or appreciates discipline? Can you identify an accomplishment or achievement in your life that came about primarily through discipline?

Have you ever incorporated spiritual disciplines (reading your Bible, prayer, etc.) into your daily routine? Have those disciplines slipped out of your routine over time? Why do you think this happens?

Spiritual Growth Self Test

Do the following statements apply to you? Answer "yes" or "no" to each.

1. I spend time daily in some form of devotional activity: prayer, Bible reading, meditating, etc.

2. I belong to a small group whose purpose includes spiritual growth.

3. I attend church regularly.

4. I have attended some type of spiritual retreat in the past year.

5. I have read at least one book in the past year whose topic dealt specifically with some aspect of the Christian life.

6. I have at least one or two close Christian friends who I trust enough to share my spiritual struggles with them or ask them to pray for me during a difficult time.

If you answered no to more than two of these questions and feel as if you are going through a "dry time" in your faith journey, consider ways to turn at least one of your no answers to a yes.

ACTION

What can you do to be consciously worshipping throughout the day?

Identify four close friends with a strong faith with whom you can form a once-a-month meeting time over lunch to support each other.

What spiritual discipline(s) can you begin to include in your everyday routine?

PRAY

:: Thank God for who He is and what He has done in your life. (Use Psalm 145)

:: Ask God to bring friends into your life with a strong faith that can keep you accountable and encourage you.

:: Pray for a close friend to grow in her relationship with the Lord.

:: Talk to God about the struggles you have with growing in your faith.

 4word®

6 Ways to Pray Throughout the Workday

NOTES

On your commute to work, ask God to prepare you for the day and to bless the work that you do.

As you walk through your office, pray for your colleagues. Ask God to bless them as they go through their day.

Before you interact with others, either in person, on the phone, or through email, ask God to guide your words. Ask Him to give you wisdom in the words that you choose and the way you speak to others.

Pray for your boss. Ask God to help her make wise decisions and be a good leader.

Pray for your colleagues who do not know the Lord. Ask God to work in their hearts and draw them to Him.

Before a performance review, ask God to give you open ears, a teachable spirit, and peace in hearing constructive criticism.

NOTES

study guide chapter 13

 4word

In what ways is your experience as a woman different from your mother's? Your grandmother's?

What would you consider a Christian stance on money and its place in marriage?

In what ways does popular culture (media, movies, etc.) reinforce the idea that your value as a person is closely tied to how much money you make? Give examples.

READ

:: Proverbs 23:4

:: Hebrews 13:5

:: 2 Corinthians 8:11

:: 1 Timothy 6:6-10, 17-19

:: Luke 14:28

:: Proverbs 24:3-4

Most experts point to money as one of the primary sources of friction in a marriage. Why do you think money causes so many arguments in marriage? How are you going to communicate openly and lovingly with each other about financial matters?

If you are married and both you and your husband are working, how do you handle your money? Who makes decisions about major purchases? How do you resolve disputes about money?

 4word

If you are married, how do you and your husband deal with business travel? How do you coordinate schedules so that one does not feel the full burden of home responsibilities?

NOTES

ACTION

What can you do to reinforce with your spouse or boyfriend that the amount of money you make is not the key ingredient for a strong relationship?

How satisfied are you with the way your husband deals with money issues? What could you both do to improve? How do you communicate about your schedules to ensure that each other is aware of the week ahead without hidden surprises?

 4word

PRAY

:: Thank God for how He continually provides for you.

:: Ask God to give you and your husband (or future husband) wisdom in being good stewards of your time and money.

:: Pray that God will give you a proper view of your value and worth in Him.

:: Talk to God about the struggles you have with financial decisions.

NOTES

God's Minimum Standards of Finance

At the end of the chapter, Diane lays out four standards that God has regarding finance. Does your financial management reflect these standards? How can you incorporate these into your financial management?

God owns everything: 1 Timothy 6:7

Think ahead and avoid problems: Luke 14:28

Keep good records: Proverbs 24:3-4

Get educated: Proverbs 14:15

4word

REFLECTION

Do you agree with the author that despite gains made by women in the workplace, it's still a man's world at work? Why or why not?

READ

:: Romans 12:16

:: Titus 2:7

:: Hebrews 10:25

:: Colossians 3:12-15

Have you ever experienced unwanted attention from men you work with? How did you deal with it? If not, do you know how you would handle that kind of situation?

How do you walk the fine line of developing strategic friendships with men without sending the wrong messages or putting yourself in an awkward position?

 4word®

NOTES

Who would be a natural, easy, beneficial, and professional person to go to and ask to be your mentor?

Romans 12:16 tells us, "Do not be proud, but be willing to associate with people of low position." Can you think of any younger women from work that you could mentor?

Titus 2:7 says, "In everything set them an example by doing what is good. In your teaching show integrity, seriousness." How can you positively influence your male co-workers by being an example of a godly woman? What are appropriate ways to interact with Christian brothers, whether in the workplace, at church, or anywhere else?

What has been your experience in trying to develop relationships with other women at work? Identify some women whom you could trust, support, receive support from, or have fun with.

ACTION

In what ways have you felt "left out" at work? What can you do to change that situation?

NOTES

Hebrews 10:25 tells us to meet with other believers to fellowship and encourage each other. Identify four to five women you would enjoy meeting with on a regular basis just to share your lives. What, if anything, is preventing you from starting such a group?

PRAY

:: Ask God for His help in trying to develop relationships with other women at your company (or in the workforce). Who can you trust, support, and receive support from or just have fun with?

:: Ask God for His help in nurturing healthy relationships with men in your company without communicating the wrong message.

:: Ask God for guidance and wisdom when dealing with unwanted attention from men at work.

:: Ask God for wisdom in how to be a godly woman in the 21st century.

6 Ways to Embrace Your Femininity at Work

Dress feminine while keeping it professional. Colors and accessories can add a feminine touch to the traditional business suit.

Connect with other women in your workplace. That camaraderie can give you the confidence to embrace your femininity in a male-dominated environment.

Show your colleagues that you care. Talk with them, ask them questions, and listen.

Create an inspiring environment. If you have an office, cubicle, or desk, decorate with a few items that inspire you: pictures, quotes, flowers, etc. These little touches can add some brightness to your space.

Walk with confidence and class.

Don't forget to smile. A smile can light up a room and ease tension in a stressful situation.

NOTES

NOTES

REFLECTION

Most research suggests that women are more likely to be perfectionists than men. Why do you think this is true?

READ

:: 2 Corinthians 12:9-10

:: Romans 6:14

:: 2 Corinthians 5:17, 21

:: 1 Thessalonians 5:18

:: Psalm 46:1

Take the "Are you a Perfectionist?" quiz on the following page. On a scale of 1 to 10 with a "10" being the mother of all perfectionists, how would you rate yourself? Give a few examples to support your score.

 4word

Are you a Perfectionist?

A lot of professional women are. If you answer "yes" to at least six of these questions, you are likely to have perfectionist tendencies:

1. I practically never leave the house—even to run a simple errand—without putting on makeup and making sure my hair is just right.

2. I find it difficult and frustrating to work with people who are not as competent or fast as I am.

3. When I finish a project successfully, I am more likely to focus on what I could have done to make it even better than to enjoy it and praise God.

4. I tend to avoid those things I'm not very good at.

5. One of my pet peeves is to come home and see clutter on the countertops in the kitchen.

6. When I receive my performance review, I tend to focus more on the "needs to improve" rather than the "exceeds standards."

7. I seldom received a grade lower than an "A" in high school and college.

8. I generally do not use self-deprecating humor; I don't enjoy being the butt of a joke.

9. If I make a mistake at work, I'm more likely to be mad at myself than to brush it off.

10. At least once in the past year, someone close to me has suggested I'm a perfectionist.

Do you feel as if you are held to higher standards at work because you are a woman? If so, who imposes those standards? Your boss? Your colleagues? You?

How are you most likely to respond to a mistake you've made? Can you think of a specific example? Describe that experience. Is there anything you can do to include God in handling the situation differently in the future?

Can you think of an example of a time you failed at something and made yourself feel like a failure? Why did you respond that way? How can you face future experiences without labeling yourself as a failure?

Diane writes that God "uses our pain to teach us more about his love for us, as he stands beside us and wraps his arms around us." What are some times in your life that have you experienced this? How did God shine brightly in your dark moments?

NOTES

ACTION

What can you do to help take the pressure of perfectionism off of you and your peers?

What fuels perfectionism in you? What do you gain by living this lifestyle? What would you lose or gain if you let it go?

1 Thessalonians 5:18 tells us to give thanks in all situations. When perfectionism tries to take hold in a situation, how can thankfulness change your perspective and the way you react?

Read "Antidotes to Perfectionism" on page 203 of Work, Love, Pray and pick something practical to do this week to curb perfectionist tendencies.

PRAY

:: Thank God for creating you and giving you the skills and gifts that allow you to work and be a good daughter, sister, wife and/or mother.

:: Are you struggling with trying to be Superwoman? If so, ask for God's help in accepting the limitations of being human and for the peace of the Holy Spirit.

:: Talk to God about any struggles you may have with perfectionist tendencies.

NOTES

REFLECTION

What were your favorite movies, songs/groups, and fashion styles when you were fifteen years old? What are they now? How have you changed as a person in that period of time? Are there characteristics and priorities at your core that haven't changed?

READ

:: Philippians 2:14-15

:: Philippians 4:6

:: Romans 8:5

:: Matthew 6:34

:: Ecclesiastes 3:10-11

How would you describe the current season of your life?

 4word

Do you feel like you are fully invested in your current season? Are you holding on to a past season or wishing away your current season for the next one?

NOTES

Have you wished away certain seasons in your life? Why?

Diane writes, "Not that they are always pleasant or easy, but change forces us to step back, reevaluate, and make adjustments that ultimately make life work better." As you move through seasons in life, have you spent time reevaluating and making adjustments? What have you learned? How have you changed from various seasons?

Is there any season in life ahead of you that you are worried about? Is there any season in life ahead of you that you are looking forward to? Explain.

Read Ecclesiastes 3:10-11. Are there seasons in your life that seemed like burdens? In retrospect, how did God make them beautiful?

In general, are you the type of person who looks forward to and embraces change, or is change difficult for you and something you try to avoid? Give an example to illustrate.

ACTION

What can you do to prepare yourself to be more graceful through change if change is difficult for you?

NOTES

Diane recommends learning from people in the next season of life. Who can you look up to who is a few seasons ahead of you?

What changes in your life have had the biggest impact on you emotionally? Spiritually? Physically? Thank God for these "seasons" in your life and His purpose behind them.

PRAY

:: Thank God for the current season you are in, even if it is difficult.

:: Ask God to help you stay content in this season of life and prepare you for the next season.

:: Pray about how you can help another woman that is a life season behind you.

:: Be honest with God about your struggles and the blessings in this current stage of life.

NOTES

4word

Do you have boundaries set to protect important areas of your life? If not, what boundaries would you like to have?

When was the last time you said no to a request for your time (whether it was from family, friends, work, or church)? How was your response received? How did you feel about saying no?

How can we, as Christians, reconcile saying no to something good?

READ

:: Matthew 6:33-34

:: Colossians 3:2

:: Mark 1:35

:: Daniel 1:8-13

:: Colossians 3:23

 4word

Is exercise a part of your routine? If so, what benefits does exercise give you? If not, why not? What are you doing to protect your health? What importance does God place on your physical well-being?

NOTES

At this stage in your career, how do you determine how much of your time to devote to volunteering or other charitable activities? Do you feel as if you should be doing more or less? Explain.

ACTION

What are you doing to establish boundaries to protect those areas of your life that are important to you? For example, do you let calls go to voice mail when it is not convenient to answer, or do you interrupt what you are doing with your family to take a call that is not important?

 4word

What do you like to do just for fun? What is most likely to prevent you from doing it? How could you create a boundary to give you more opportunities to do this? Can you combine what you like to do for fun with time with your husband, kids or a friend?

NOTES

What can you do this week to set and observe your boundaries?

PRAY

:: Think about your priorities in life. Does how you are spending your time each day and each week reflect faith as being a priority in your life?

:: Ask for God's help in creating boundaries so you can spend more time with Him.

:: Ask God for wisdom in managing your time and knowing when to rest.

:: Thank God for the blessing of work and ask Him how you can do your work "as unto the Lord."

NOTES

4word

REFLECTION

Do you believe that your work is a calling from God?

READ

:: Matthew 11:28-30

:: Romans 12:4-8

:: Psalm 139:13-16

Doing good, honest work glorifies the Lord. How are you glorifying your Maker in your work?

In what ways do you think God has guided your steps in the workforce and in life?

 4word

What abilities has God entrusted to you? How are you using them?

Are you investing your time and energy in things that are consistent with your values and beliefs?

ACTION

Look at "Ebby's secrets of success" list:

- Develop a daily relationship with God

- Stay healthy

- Keep learning

- Leave a positive impression

- Express gratitude

- Choose your partner carefully

- Contribute to your community

How do you currently live out these practices? Which ones are struggles for you? What can you practically do to grow in these areas?

Frances Hesselbein says her life's motto is "to serve is to live." How can you live out that statement this week?

PRAY

:: Thank God for giving you skills to grow in the professional world and for preparing you for your current position.

:: Look at God's hand and guidance in your life. Thank Him for directing you.

:: Ask God how you can serve other professional women around you.

:: Ask God to help you do excellent work as an offering to the Lord, because it's what Christ deserves.

:: Talk to God about being highly intentional about our spiritual influence and being wise, winsome witnesses in our place of work.

NOTES

connect with 4word

LOCAL GROUPS ::

4word connects women face to face with others who feel called to use their God-given talents in the workplace. Local groups are forming all over the country.

Log on to 4wordwomen.org/cities, or email localgroups@4wordwomen.org to find a group near you.

DIGITAL PLATFORMS ::

   Like us on Facebook at 4word

   Follow us on Twitter @4word

   Connect with us on LinkedIn at 4word

   Join us on Google+ at 4word

   Follow us on Pinterest at 4word

   Follow us on Instagram at 4wordwomen

   Find us on YouTube at 4wordwomen

Credits:

Avery Dale

Diane Paddison, 4word Founder and CEO

Sandra Crawford Williamson, 4word COO

Katie Reiff, 4word Director

Betsy Gray Creative Group

Lyn Cook

Peter Battaglia for advising on relevant Scripture reference.

Natalie Snyder and Brenda Ridnour for chapter content.

Cover photo: Faceout Studio

NOTES

NOTES

Work, Love, Pray

NOTES

110

NOTES

"For we are God's handiwork, created in Christ Jesus to do good works, which God prepared in advance for us to do."

:: Ephesians 2:10 ::